Francis Frith's
DEVON

PHOTOGRAPHIC MEMORIES

Francis Frith's
DEVON

Dennis Needham

FRITH
BOOK Co

First published in the United Kingdom in 1999 by
Frith Book Company Ltd

British Library Cataloguing in Publication Data

Devon
Dennis Needham
ISBN 1-85937-052-7

Frith Book Company Ltd
Frith's Barn, Teffont,
Salisbury, Wiltshire SP3 5QP
Tel: +44 (0) 1722 716 376
Email: frithbook.co.uk

Printed and bound in Great Britain

Contents

Francis Frith: Victorian Pioneer 7

Frith's Archive - A Unique Legacy 10

Devon - An Introduction 12

The South Coast 16

The Towns 50

The Cities 71

The County's Backwaters 86

The North Coast 100

Index 122

Free Mounted Print Voucher 123

Francis Frith: *Victorian Pioneer*

Francis Frith, Victorian founder of the world-famous photographic archive, was a complex and multitudinous man. A devout Quaker and a highly successful Victorian businessman, he was both philosophic by nature and pioneering in outlook.

By 1855 Francis Frith had already established a wholesale grocery business in Liverpool, and sold it for the astonishing sum of £200,000, which is the equivalent today of over £15,000,000. Now a multi-millionaire, he was able to indulge his passion for travel. As a child he had pored over travel books written by early explorers, and his fancy and imagination had been stirred by family holidays to the sublime mountain regions of Wales and Scotland. 'What a land of spirit-stirring and enriching scenes and places!' he had written. He was to return to these scenes of grandeur in later years to 'recapture the thousands of vivid and tender memories', but with a different purpose. Now in his thirties, and captivated by the new science of photography, Frith set out on a series of pioneering journeys to the Nile regions that occupied him from 1856 until 1860.

Intrigue and Adventure

He took with him on his travels a specially-designed wicker carriage that acted as both dark-room and sleeping chamber. These far-flung journeys were packed with intrigue and adventure. In his life story, written when he was sixty-three, Frith tells of being held captive by bandits, and of fighting 'an awful midnight battle to the very point of surrender with a deadly pack of hungry, wild dogs'. Sporting flowing Arab costume, Frith arrived at Akaba by camel seventy years before Lawrence, where he encountered 'desert princes and rival sheikhs, blazing with jewel-hilted swords'.

During these extraordinary adventures he was assiduously exploring the desert regions bordering the Nile and patiently recording the antiquities and peoples with his camera. He was the first photographer to venture beyond the sixth cataract. Africa was still the mysterious 'Dark Continent', and Stanley and Livingstone's historic meeting was a decade into the future. The conditions for picture taking confound belief. He laboured for hours in his wicker dark-room in the sweltering heat of the desert, while the volatile chemicals fizzed dangerously in their trays. Often he was forced to work in remote tombs and caves where conditions were cooler. Back in London he exhibited his photographs and was 'rapturously cheered' by members of the Royal Society. His reputation as a photographer was made overnight. An eminent modern historian has likened their impact on the population of the time to that on our own generation of the first photographs taken on the surface of the moon.

VENTURE OF A LIFE-TIME

Characteristically, Frith quickly spotted the opportunity to create a new business as a specialist publisher of photographs. He lived in an era of immense and sometimes violent change. For the poor in the early part of Victoria's reign work was a drudge and the hours long, and people had precious little free time to enjoy themselves.

Most had no transport other than a cart or gig at their disposal, and had not travelled far beyond the boundaries of their own town or village. However, by the 1870s, the railways had threaded their way across the country, and Bank Holidays and half-day Saturdays had been made obligatory by Act of Parliament. All of a sudden the ordinary working man and his family were able to enjoy days out and see a little more of the world.

With characteristic business acumen, Francis Frith foresaw that these new tourists would enjoy having souvenirs to commemorate their days out. In 1860 he married Mary Ann Rosling and set out with the intention of photographing every city, town and village in Britain. For the next thirty years he travelled the country by train and by pony and trap, producing fine photographs of seaside resorts and beauty spots that were keenly bought by millions of Victorians. These prints were painstakingly pasted into family albums and pored over during the dark nights of winter, rekindling precious memories of summer excursions.

THE RISE OF FRITH & CO

Frith's studio was soon supplying retail shops all over the country. To meet the demand he gathered about him a small team of photographers, and published the work of independent artist-photographers of the calibre of Roger Fenton and Francis Bedford. In order to gain some understanding of the scale of Frith's business one only has to look at the catalogue issued by Frith & Co in 1886: it runs to some 670

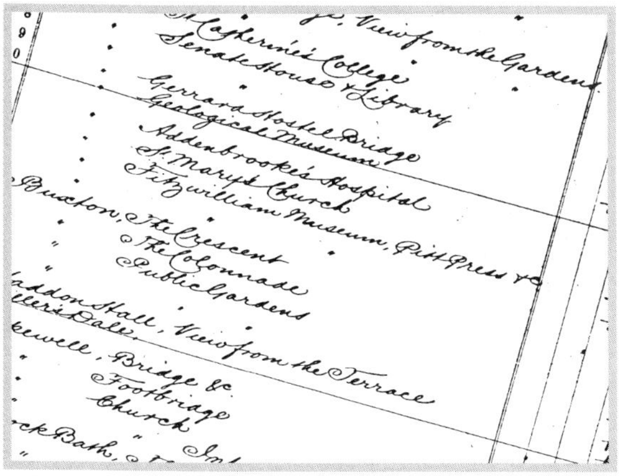

pages, listing not only many thousands of views of the British Isles but also many photographs of most European countries, and China, Japan, the USA and Canada – note the sample page shown above from the hand-written *Frith & Co* ledgers detailing pictures taken. By 1890 Frith had created the greatest specialist photographic publishing company in the world, with over 2,000 outlets – more than the combined number that Boots and WH Smith have today! The picture on the right shows the *Frith & Co* display board at Ingleton in the Yorkshire Dales. Beautifully constructed with mahogany frame and gilt inserts, it could display up to a dozen local scenes.

Postcard Bonanza

The ever-popular holiday postcard we know today took many years to develop. In 1870 the Post Office issued the first plain cards, with a pre-printed stamp on one face. In 1894 they allowed other publishers' cards to be sent through the mail with an attached adhesive halfpenny stamp. Demand grew rapidly, and in 1895 a new size of postcard was permitted called the court card, but there was little room for illustration. In 1899, a year after Frith's death, a new card measuring 5.5 x 3.5 inches became the standard format, but it was not until 1902 that the divided back came into being, with address and message on one face and a full-size illustration on the other. *Frith & Co* were in the vanguard of postcard development, and Frith's sons Eustace and Cyril continued their father's monumental task, expanding the number of views offered to the public and recording more and more places in Britain, as the coasts and countryside were opened up to mass travel.

Francis Frith died in 1898 at his villa in Cannes, his great project still growing. The archive he created continued in business for another seventy years. By 1970 it contained over a third of a million pictures of 7,000 cities, towns and villages. The massive photographic record Frith has left to us stands as a living monument to a special and very remarkable man.

Frith's Archive: *A Unique Legacy*

Francis Frith's legacy to us today is of immense significance and value, for the magnificent archive of evocative photographs he created provides a unique record of change in 7,000 cities, towns and villages throughout Britain over a century and more. Frith and his fellow studio photographers revisited locations many times down the years to update their views, compiling for us an enthralling and colourful pageant of British life and character.

We tend to think of Frith's sepia views of Britain as nostalgic, for most of us use them to conjure up memories of places in our own lives with which we have family associations. It often makes us forget that to Francis Frith they were records of daily life as it was actually being lived in the cities, towns and villages of his day. The Victorian age was one of great and often bewildering change for ordinary people, and though the pictures evoke an impression of slower times, life was as busy and hectic as it is today.

We are fortunate that Frith was a photographer of the people, dedicated to recording the minutiae of everyday life. For it is this sheer wealth of visual data, the painstaking chronicle of changes in dress, transport, street layouts, buildings, housing, engineering and landscape that captivates us so much today. His remarkable images offer us a powerful link with the past and with the lives of our ancestors.

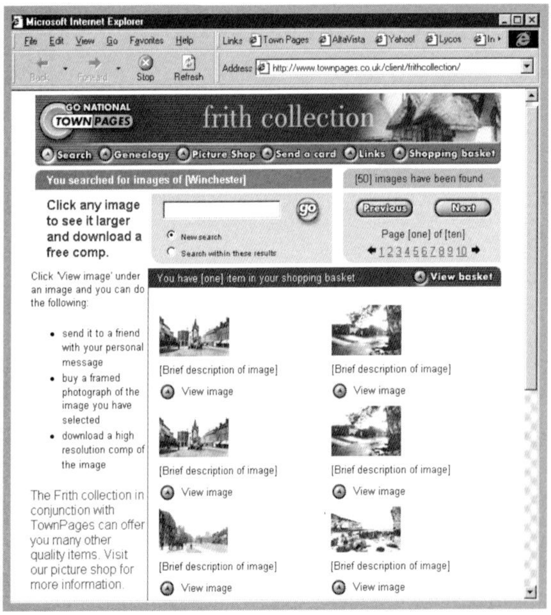

See Frith at www. francisfrith.co.uk

Today's Technology

Computers have now made it possible for Frith's many thousands of images to be accessed almost instantly. In the Frith archive today, each photograph is carefully 'digitised' then stored on a CD Rom. Frith archivists can locate a single photograph amongst thousands within seconds. Views can be catalogued and sorted under a variety of categories of place and content to the immediate benefit of researchers. Inexpensive reference prints can be created for them at the touch of a mouse button, and a wide range of books and other printed materials assembled and published for a wider, more general readership - in the next twelve months over a hundred Frith local history titles will be published! The day-to-day workings of the archive are very different from how they were in Francis Frith's time: imagine the herculean task of sorting through eleven tons of glass negatives as Frith had to do to locate a particular sequence of pictures! Yet the archive still prides itself on maintaining the same high standards of excellence laid down by Francis Frith, including the painstaking cataloguing and indexing of every view.

It is curious to reflect on how the internet now allows researchers in America and elsewhere greater instant access to the archive than Frith himself ever enjoyed. Many thousands of individual views can be called up on screen within seconds on one of the Frith internet sites, enabling people living continents away to revisit the streets of their ancestral home town, or view places in Britain where they have enjoyed holidays. Many overseas researchers welcome the chance to view special theme selections, such as transport, sports, costume and ancient monuments.

We are certain that Francis Frith would have heartily approved of these modern developments, for he himself was always working at the very limits of Victorian photographic technology.

The Value of the Archive Today

Because of the benefits brought by the computer, Frith's images are increasingly studied by social historians, by researchers into genealogy and ancestory, by architects, town planners, and by teachers and schoolchildren involved in local history projects. In addition, the archive offers every one of us a unique opportunity to examine the places where we and our families have lived and worked down the years. Immensely successful in Frith's own era, the archive is now, a century and more on, entering a new phase of popularity.

The Past in Tune with the Future

Historians consider the Francis Frith Collection to be of prime national importance. It is the only archive of its kind remaining in private ownership and has been valued at a million pounds. However, this figure is now rapidly increasing as digital technology enables more and more people around the world to enjoy its benefits.

Francis Frith's archive is now housed in an historic timber barn in the beautiful village of Teffont in Wiltshire. Its founder would not recognize the archive office as it is today. In place of the many thousands of dusty boxes containing glass plate negatives and an all-pervading odour of photographic chemicals, there are now ranks of computer screens. He would be amazed to watch his images travelling round the world at unimaginable speeds through network and internet lines.

The archive's future is both bright and exciting. Francis Frith, with his unshakeable belief in making photographs available to the greatest number of people, would undoubtedly approve of what is being done today with his lifetime's work. His photographs, depicting our shared past, are now bringing pleasure and enlightenment to millions around the world a century and more after his death.

Devon – *An Introduction*

TUCKED AWAY in the west country of England, the county of Devon is often regarded as little more than a holiday destination, but the county has a rich historical heritage that can inspire and delight the visitor.

For years, Devon was the second largest county in England. Then, in 1974, boundaries were redrawn and the largest county, Yorkshire, was divided into three separate units. But that did not make Devon the largest county, for in the north, Cumberland and Westmorland were combined to form Cumbria, and so Devon remained runner-up. The population of just over a million is concentrated in the south of the county, where its two great cities, Exeter and Plymouth, are located. There is also the 'Riviera Coast' to the south, which centres on Torquay. The north of the county was a rural backwater until the 1980s, when a new road was built linking the M5 motorway with Barnstaple. This re-opened routes to such places as Ilfracombe and Bideford, which had lost their rail services and had been quite remote until then.

Tourism brings considerable prosperity to the county. But Devon has a surprising diversity of commercial activity as well. Agriculture is another important part of the county's economy, with both sheep and dairy farming figuring prominently. In the wilderness of Dartmoor, and the larger part of Exmoor within the county boundary, arable potential is limited. But to the east, the red soil produces potatoes, and by the end of each summer there are fields of golden cereal crops awaiting the attention of the harvester. Mining also plays a role. Kaolin and ball clay are produced from rich beds in both the south and west of the county. Much of this is exported, with Teignmouth the busiest port in Devon. Bideford is also still an active port, with ships going to the continent, and especially to Spain. Honiton lace and Dartington glass are two of the more specialised craft industries of Devon.

Cider is another craft activity; only one sizeable producer remains in Winkleigh. What is produced there is of the highest quality and should be approached with caution by the inexperienced. What might appear a delicious lunchtime pint can leave your legs developing a mind of their own, while an overpowering desire to sleep manifests itself.

The cream tea - scones, jam and Devonshire cream - is another of the county's delights: never, however, call it 'clotted cream', for the manufacturing processes involved in making clotted cream in Cornwall and Devonshire cream are different. Cornwall scalds only the cream, and Devon the whole of the milk.

The scenery of this most gentle of counties is of an almost infinite variety. The lush green pastures of the Exe Valley around Cullompton are in striking contrast to the stark tors of Dartmoor. The river Tamar, dividing Cornwall and Devon for much of its length, has muddy flats at the lower end, wooded slopes higher up and craggy promontories on each side. The bridges that cross this river are sheer poetry to the eye. The Saltash railway bridge, designed by the great Isambard Kingdom Brunel, was an engineering wonder when it was built. The Saltash Road Bridge alongside carries more people today, but does not compete for beauty with Brunel's masterpiece. A little higher up the Tamar, another railway crossing at Calstock sweeps elegantly across the water. The train ride from Exeter to Newton Abbot is a memorable experience. Along the estuary of the Exe and beside the sea wall to Dawlish are major wintering habitats for migratory birds. Several short tunnels are linked by another wall, which is frequently damaged by winter storms roaring up the English Channel. Many a train has had a severe salt washing while travelling along this section, which is one of the most spectacular in the country. For lovers of sheer beauty, Lydford Gorge is essential. A short walk up the gorge reveals a waterfall almost 100ft high, steep ravines, the Devil's Cauldron whirlpool and some ancient oak woods.

But Devon is nothing if not a seafaring county. It has produced many of our most famous sailors. Francis Drake was born near Tavistock, and Walter Raleigh near Sidmouth. That most famous of paintings, 'The Boyhood of Raleigh', was painted by Sir John Millais on the sea wall at Budleigh Salterton. All around its coasts small boats put out to sea, trying to wrest a living from the often unfriendly waters. Big ships are to be seen, too. Plymouth is a major ferry port with daily sailings to Roscoff in Brittany and regular crossings to

Santander in northern Spain. The Navy are always active in Plymouth Sound, making the city a ship-spotter's paradise. Another of Devon's famous rivers is the Dart. Rising in Dartmoor Forest, it flows for 36 miles south towards the English Channel. At its southern end, the river is a magnet for yachtsmen. Pleasure boats also ply the river from Dartmouth and Kingswear up to Totnes. On this section of river, near Dittisham, the writer of detective thrillers, Agatha Christie, lived until her death in 1976.

The north of Devon is altogether more rugged. Cliffs and jagged rocks thrusting out into the sea make this a most inhospitable coastline. From the north-facing shore of Lynmouth as far as Ilfracombe, there is little refuge. Lynmouth now presents a calm face. But disastrous events on 15 August 1952 brought the village to the world's notice. It had been a particularly wet August, and Exmoor, high above the village, was waterlogged. Then a 22-hour period of heavy rain culminating in an enormous thunderstorm created nine more inches of rain by that Friday night. It ran straight off the land, flooding the East and West Lyn rivers. Some years before, where the twin rivers meet in Lynmouth, the West Lyn had been diverted and culverted into the East river, which it joined at right angles. But that night the culverts were blocked, and the East and West rivers came together in a boiling, angry torrent. A wall of water crashed through Lynmouth, spreading across the delta and wreaking destruction on everything in its path. By dawn on Saturday, the water level had dropped and the true extent of the devastation was revealed. Thirty-four people had died, dozens were homeless and a similar number of buildings were damaged or demolished. Today, there is little evidence of the ferocity and horror of that night, and the beautiful twin rivers run safely.

Ilfracombe is one of the departure points for the ferry to Lundy, a delightful island 18 miles out in the Bristol Channel. The other departure point for Lundy is Bideford on the river Torridge. The estuary here, where Torridge meets Taw, is a popular holiday spot.

There are many lovely old villages. Appledore offers a nostalgic mixture of fishermen's cottages, pubs and narrow winding lanes. Along the coast to the west is the picturesque and justly famous village of Clovelly. Here wreckers used to ply their evil trade. Lanterns were tied to a donkey's tail and the beast was encouraged to walk along the cliff top. Mistaking this moving light for another ship, a captain would assume that this was a safe haven, with fatal results.

The Torbay coast draws the most visitors because of its scenic beauty and temperate climate. There are 22 miles of coastline from St Mary's Bay to Maidencombe. Torquay itself is a mass of hotels and guest houses. It acquired a certain cachet in the last century when the Napoleonic wars prevented people from travelling abroad. The extent and form of the town was established in those long-gone days. If Torquay is sophisticated, Paignton is a little more brash. Most of the town is given over to holidaymakers. One building of architectural interest is Oldway Mansion, built in 1873 by the Singer sewing machine owner. It is partially modelled on the Paris Opera House. The drama of the architecture was mirrored by the scandal caused when the American dancer Isadora Duncan came to live in the house with Singer's son. Steam train enthusiasts will enjoy Paignton. Alongside the station is the start of a private railway to Kingswear. The old Great Western line was a popular route and offered one anomaly: the railway company built a station in Dartmouth, but there were no trains to serve it. Passengers came down to Kingswear and then crossed the river on a ferry.

The South Coast

MENTION South Devon and the image in many minds is of golden sands around the Torbay area, Exeter Cathedral and Dartmoor. But the area has so much more to offer. The South Hams, with a thousand small coves and tiny beaches, is an area where you can still discover peace away from the hordes of visitors. Dartmouth, famed for the Britannia Royal Naval College, boasts 800 years of history. The nearby Bayard's Cove brought the area even greater fame when the television series 'The Onedin Line' was filmed there. Salcombe, at the water's edge, is a maze of streets, but traffic-free. An almost land-locked harbour, it is a magnet for yachts. Blackpool Sands, Torcross and Slapton offer the kind of beach you might enjoy in Torbay but without the crowds. Torbay, peaceful today, once echoed to the sound of an army in action as the D-Day Normandy landings were rehearsed there.

Heading east, the stretch between Teignmouth and Dawlish offers a diverse landscape of coast and cliff, town and country. Teignmouth keeps its industrial port well concealed from the visitor behind the entrance to the river Teign. A stroll along the coast towards Holcombe is a delight, as the pier and amusements give way to peace and quiet - apart from the trains racing through alongside the path.

The town is a mass of ancient buildings. A ferry ride across the estuary brings you to Shaldon, another small village that would bring today's town planners nightmares, with its riot of buildings seemingly heaped one on top of the other.

Further east, Budleigh Salterton is an exquisite town with a pebble beach, offering stunning coastal views in both directions. The cliffs continue to dominate, giving little access to the shore until Sidmouth is reached. The town clings to the sides of a valley formed by the river Sid, with the hills around revealing beautiful views out to sea. It is a gruelling ten mile walk along the cliffs to Seaton Bay, but again the views are breathtaking. Beer is a small village, which although it is linked with Seaton, has its own unique character and identity. Seaton is a popular holiday spot, with caravan sites to house the thousands of visitors coming here each year. Seaton, once a cluster of houses in the middle of nowhere, grew because it was a junction on the Southern Railway's London to Exeter line. Although the railway has gone, an enterprising company opened a tramway using much of the old track bed. This offers a delightful ride up the Axe Valley to Colyton. So this, then, is the glorious county of Devon. Those who live here generally seem happy to forgo the more sophisticated aspects of modern living for a life of pleasure in a temperate climate. They are also remarkably sanguine about life, pointing out that although the major centres of population are often at least two hours away, the natural beauty and relaxed lifestyle is more than adequate compensation.

Beer, The Village 1892 31318

In 1892, there were acres of thatch to see in Beer, as well as unsurfaced roads. Today, the place is still delightful, and has better roads. This was a typical Devon seaside community where smuggling was endemic. One of Devon's most notorious smugglers, Jack Rattenbury, lived locally two centuries ago.

Beer, The Beach 1898 42434

There were plenty of fishing boats in what used to be known as Beer Roads. The rocky promontory, East Ebb, divided Seaton from Beer and kept the two places apart. The many caves in the cliffs offered smugglers discreet hideaways.

BEER, THE VILLAGE 1922 72946

The parish church of St Michael was built in 1878 on the site of an older chapel. Beer is famed for its quarries, which were worked by the Romans and have continued in use down the years. The stone was used extensively for the arcades of many Devon churches.

BEER, PILLOW LACE WORKERS 1901 47861

Lace was made in east Devon. Here, in a rather posed photograph, a well-dressed family stand outside a pleasant house in Beer with lace being worked in the foreground. Although Honiton is the accepted centre, there were 500 lace workers in Beer in 1850.

Sidmouth, The Esplanade 1918 68739

The red sandstone cliffs in the picture rise to 500ft on either side of the river Sid's valley. The town was one of many that became popular during the Napoleonic wars when the rich could not travel to Europe. They found Sidmouth before Torquay and it developed accordingly.

Sidmouth, Looking West 1924 76360

Again, the cliffs stand out in the background. As the railway did not arrive until 1874, the town remained unspoilt by mass tourism, especially as the beach was shingle. Thus the mansions, built earlier, were not ruined and much of the town remains old-fashioned, untouched by modern development.

C.A.MAEER
C. BERWICK

SIDMOUTH

Fore Street 1904 52071

The town's busy shopping street brims with traditional small shops with multi-paned frontages and painted signboards. The streets are narrow and congested with coaches and carts, even before the car made any impression on the place.

SIDMOUTH, HIGH STREET 1906 53807

SIDMOUTH
High Street 1906
That the area is not disfigured by Victorian brickwork is an indication of how slowly the town developed. The varied facades create a flowing and pleasing harmony. Only the parish church suffered, being almost completely rebuilt in 1859 in a rather plain style.

SIDMOUTH
West End 1904
An indication of the lack of visitors to Sidmouth can be gleaned from this picture, taken from the Esplanade. The sea wall was constructed in 1835 and the shingle beach can be clearly seen. Overlooking the sea are some fine old cottages, exuberant in design and with bulging thatch.

SIDMOUTH, WEST END 1904 52069

BUDLEIGH SALTERTON, THE PROMENADE 1898 42448
The sea wall is the one featured in that most evocative of paintings, 'The Boyhood of Raleigh', painted by Sir John Millais when he was resident in the town.

BUDLEIGH SALTERTON, HIGH STREET 1898 42453
As a seaside town, Budleigh has developed almost entirely since the beginning of the eighteenth century. It was known as Saltre in 1210, and had become Salterne by 1405. The names were derived from the salt pans, which were located on the river Otter.

BUDLEIGH SALTERTON, HIGH STREET 1918 68726

This picture shows a scene similar to the previous view, but was taken a little further up the street and 20 years later. The main street is still peaceful in character, and the many visitors would have been crowded onto the red pebble beach at the far end.

Exmouth, The Sands 1890 26261

Exmouth is reputed to be the oldest seaside town in Devon. People from Exeter used the sea and sands, the only good bathing beach in the east, back in the early seventeenth century. This view of the beach shows it in use by both holidaymakers and local fishermen.

Exmouth, View from the Beacon 1925 78594

The river Exe from Beacon Hill. This fashionable area was home to Lady Nelson after her estrangement from the Admiral. By the time this picture was taken, the holiday business was well established. The high ground in the distance is the edge of Dartmoor.

TOPSHAM

The Quay 1906 53990

Topsham, on the river Exe, is truly ancient. The Romans used it as their port to service Exeter, a function it continued to provide for centuries. By the date of this picture, its working days were over, leaving a pleasant riverside town, well loved for its ornate architecture.

DAWLISH, BLENHEIM HOTEL 1925 78435

This is 'new' Dawlish, built after a replacement sea wall had allowed the shoreside area to be reclaimed from the sea. The sweep of the sandy bay and the railway along the shore are clearly visible here. The Blenheim Hotel, shown in the centre, is now converted to holiday flats: a sign of the times.

DAWLISH, BOAT COVE 1925 78437

A view showing the new part of Dawlish, taken from Boat Cove. The sea front remains largely unchanged, with its villas and small hotels. The building to the right is the railway station, exposed to everything an English Channel storm can throw at it. In severe weather, services are disrupted.

DAWLISH
The Strand 1928
As can be seen, Dawlish Water was straightened and landscaped along a series of attractive small waterfalls. Immensely popular in the eighteenth century, Jane Austen and Charles Dickens knew and loved the town. They would both recognize it today. Dickens used the town as the birthplace of Nicholas Nickleby.

DAWLISH
The Beach 1922
A typically busy picture of Dawlish beach. The rich variety of reds in the sandstone cliff are a delight to the eye. Brunel's seaside railway runs in and out of the cliffs through five narrow tunnels, offering a breathtaking ride for travellers to Paignton and Torquay.

DAWLISH, THE STRAND 1928 81171

DAWLISH, THE BEACH 1922 72990

TEIGNMOUTH, FROM TORQUAY ROAD 1890 26021
An overview of Teignmouth, taken from Shaldon Hill, across the estuary of the river Teign. The town is said to be Devon's oldest resort. The commercial port was, and is, to the left of the picture where vessels of the era appear. The navigation channel is so unstable that pilots check it after each tide.

TEIGNMOUTH, THE TERRACE WALK 1911 63698
Current fashions are well displayed in this photograph. The Walk continues north towards Dawlish for nearly two miles, the sea on one side, the railway on the other. On the left is an imposing villa, remarkably restrained in character for the seaside, with its decorative motifs from classical architecture.

TEIGNMOUTH, FROM THE PIER 1903 49560

This photograph shows the holiday season in full swing. The bathing huts will soon be winched down to the shallows so that modest ladies can paddle discreetly. It is surprising to learn that the town was bombed repeatedly during the last war and an amazing 3% of the population were casualties.

BABBACOMBE, THE DOWNS 1918 68547
A popular clifftop band concert at Babbacombe. Once a small village, Babbacombe has long been subsumed into Torquay and struggles to keep its own identity. This picture shows the view north towards Teignmouth. Here, a crowd enjoys the music of the band wafting through the warm sea air.

BABBACOMBE, THE BEACH 1925 78445
The virtual lack of sand kept families away from this section of coast, which is brilliant with white pebbles. John Keats was enchanted with the waterside scenery at Babbacombe when he visited, and declared that it offered the finest prospects he had seen in Devon.

Torquay, Anstey's Cove 1896 38609
This quiet little corner is on the north side of Torquay and reached by way of a romantic wooded ravine. There is no beach here, but the Victorians were determined to make the most of the warm waters. The bathing machine, sunk to its axles in the shallows, allowed decorum to be preserved.

Torquay, The Beach 1924 76401
Torquay has long been a magnet for holidaymakers from all over the country. Its gentle climate in all seasons has proved irresistible. Styled as the English Riviera, its beaches are in fact somewhat smaller than might be imagined. This crowded scene looks south along Torbay towards Paignton. Changing tents have replaced the earlier bathing machines.

TORQUAY, FLEET STREET 1906 54027
The ladies are dressed fashionably, but in the event of a storm the road surface would turn quickly into a quagmire which would surely dirty their smart clothes. A motor vehicle is approaching the camera, but the horse still reigns supreme. In the background newly-built villas speckle the wooded slopes.

TORQUAY, A FARMYARD SCENE 1906 54016
The grace of Fleet Street in the previous picture is counterpointed by the timeless nature of this rural view, taken the same year on the outskirts of Torquay, possibly at Cockington. Tumbrils and carts have been stored under a thatched shed, its ground floor open to the elements. To the right is a sizeable dung pile.

PAIGNTON, THE PROMENADE AND SANDS 1907 58415A

The promenade and beach are thronged with visitors. The ungainly motor vehicle in the centre is still an unusual enough feature for it to be attracting the attention of bystanders. A small cluster of brightly-striped bathing machines can be seen at the water's edge. By the time of the Great War they were obsolete.

Paignton

Preston Sands 1918 68533

Presumably, these Avro 504J float-planes caused a considerable stir when they arrived. They were part of a batch of 200 built by Avro for the Royal Flying Corps in 1916 and still carry their military markings, although the name on the side indicates some form of civilian activity.

PAIGNTON, CHURCH STREET 1912 64719
Pook Brothers' butcher's shop, on the right, has a fine display of meat that would throw today's health inspectors into an immediate lather. St John's parish church was rebuilt in the fifteenth century, although the pinnacled tower is twelfth century.

PAIGNTON, THE BATHING BEACH 1896 38545
Bathing machines were designed to be pushed into the sea, allowing bathers to change and enter the water with maximum decorum. It is curious to think that a generation earlier, nude bathing, at least by the gentlemen, was completely accepted. The Yorkshire resort of Scarborough claims to have invented these machines.

BRIXHAM, THE PRINCE OF ORANGE MONUMENT 1891 28241
Brixham is located at the south end of Tor Bay. Its natural harbour, sheltered by the limestone cliffs, made it ideal for settlement. The Saxons were here, and Celtic and Roman remains have been found nearby. The statue on the left, commemorating the landing here by William of Orange on 5 November 1688, was erected in 1891.

BRIXHAM, THE FISHING FLEET 1896 38893
Before being overtaken by Plymouth a couple of decades earlier, Brixham was the leading fishing port in Devon. At one time, there were almost 300 trawlers employing 1600 seamen. Hundreds more workers on shore built and repaired the ships and manufactured sails and clothing, whilst the women knitted underwea and packed the fish.

BRIXHAM, THE INNER HARBOUR 1906 54039
Fishing boats squat in the harbour mud. At one time, the waters stretched another half-mile inland, but the land has been filled in and built on. The wholesale fish market at Brixham was the largest in the west of England at this time.

Brixham
Fore Street 1922
Because the town had been so heavily dependent on the single industry of fishing, the Depression of the 1930s arrived in Brixham early. It was fortunate that its popularity as a holiday destination brought it a welcome alternative source of income.

Brixham
Bolton Cross 1922
Both the Town Hall, the stone building on the right, and the Bolton Hotel on the left, are still here today. Bolton Cross is a local name given to the meeting of Bolton Street, New Road, Middle Street and Fore Street. Children gather around the public drinking fountain.

Brixham, Fore Street 1922 73032

Brixham, Bolton Cross 1922 73033

Brixham

The Harbour 1925 78490

After 1919, the fishing industry failed. Men returning from the war had only old boats, and the price of fish collapsed. In 1919 there were 120 boats, but by 1936, just six. A varied collection of roadsters and three-wheelers encircle the harbour. In the background is a charabanc.

DARTMOUTH, NEW QUAY 1890 25289
'New' Quay was actually built in 1585. Before that, ships tied up at the churchyard wall of St Saviour's, the tower of which, built in 1631, can be seen in the centre. The Castle Hotel, with its imposing castellated frontage, dominates the waterfront. Dartmouth was once one of England's greatest ports, exporting wool and cloth.

DARTMOUTH, THE ROYAL NAVAL COLLEGE 1918 68612A
This masterpiece of grand architecture was built (1902-05) by Sir Aston Webb, who was also responsible for the eastern façade of Buckingham Palace and for Admiralty Arch, both in London. Its vast red and white façade, cradled by trees, looms over the town. It was opened by Edward VII.

DITTISHAM, ON THE DART 1889 21617
The Dart was once a river busy with commercial traffic, including great steamships. Poor rail services saw these vessels diverted to Southampton so that the mails could be more speedily dealt with. Dittisham and Dartmouth now rely on the leisure industry, and are the haunt of weekend yachtsmen.

SALCOMBE, THE QUAYSIDE 1896 38483

SALCOMBE
The Quayside 1896

A sailing ship is discharging its cargo alongside the quay with its cluster of warehouses. Until relatively recent times, the sea was a vital artery for supplying the town. In late summer the pilchard shoals would arrive and the town was a bustle of small boats. During other months the fishermen caught lobsters and crabs.

SALCOMBE
from Portlemouth 1928

Salcombe was preserved from wholesale development because it was never reached by the railway. Kingsbridge, five miles to the north, was the closest the line ever penetrated. With only a small beach to boast of it never attracted hordes of holidaymakers. The 19th century church (right) is Holy Trinity.

SALCOMBE, FROM PORTLEMOUTH 1928 81014

SALCOMBE, FORE STREET 1907 58775
The Shipwright's Arms on the left is still open for business, and its name gives an indication of one of the old trades in town - until the late years of Victoria's reign the town's main industry was the building of schooners.

HOPE COVE, THE COTTAGES 1890 25260

Hope is one of the more remote corners of Devon, located on the west side of the South Hams, six miles from Kingsbridge. With only one narrow lane to provide access, it has retained its unspoilt nature. This photograph, with its old white cottages with their tumbling thatch, reveals Hope's unchanging face.

HOPE COVE, THE BEACH AND VILLAGE 1925 78392

The two parts of the village are Inner Hope and Outer Hope. There had once been a small fishing fleet here that worked the huge pilchard shoals that congregated in Bigbury Bay. Those halcyon days were long gone when this picture was taken.

Bovisand, The Harbour 1925 78508

The tiny harbour of Bovisand. Another inaccessible corner of the county, this is only a few miles from Plymouth, opposite the breakwater in Plymouth Sound. Here, a boat packed with holidaymakers has returned from a trip to view the distant prospects of Plymouth and the Hoe.

Bovisand, The Landing Steps 1925 78509

The main use of the harbour appears to be for recreation. A few fishing boats once worked in the area, but there are no signs of them in this photograph, just a small pleasure boat. The harbour has no picturesque buildings and retains its old working character.

The Towns

THE TOPOGRAPHY of Devon lends itself to smaller towns and villages. Only Exeter and Plymouth, with Roman and naval connections respectively, are centres of population. For the rest, the sleepy market town with its long history is archetypal Devon. With a population of around one million (Surrey has a similar figure in less than a quarter of the space), Devon continues to be a rural county where people wish to live and retire. This is making for fundamental demographic change, although the basic shape of the towns and villages remains unaltered. So although some towns have tended to grow, this has generally been at the periphery, and their ancient hearts remain much as they were.

With the vast expanse of Dartmoor, some 140,000 acres, taking up a sizeable proportion of the county, areas for the towns to be located in the first place were a little restricted. We find Totnes, Newton Abbot and Tavistock in the south, Barnstaple and Great Torrington in the north and Okehampton and Tiverton in the centre. With Honiton in the east, these are the only 'major' centres of population. Each has its own individual characteristics. Okehampton lies in the shadow of the Moor, and much of its activity reflects this. Search and Rescue teams are based there, and the army, which uses large areas of the moor for manoeuvres.

Tavistock, also in the shadow of Dartmoor, was once a great copper and tin mining centre, and there are still traces of this industrial heritage. Honiton was, and is, famous for lace, although the industry is a mere shadow of its former self. Totnes is probably the most ancient of these towns. There are records of a Saxon village here, and at one time the place issued its own coinage, as did Barnstaple. Apart from agriculture, the woollen industry thrived here for centuries, trading with foreign countries. Both Barnstaple's Castle Quay and Rolle Quay were major centres of activity. However, after the river silted up only the shallowest draughted vessels can reach the town today.

Newton Abbot has probably seen the largest increase in population since the railways arrived. Its location meant that several railways met there, and it became an important railway junction. Ball clay deposits are located close to the town, offering local employment. Tiverton developed in the 15th century when kersey manufacture was begun. This coarse cloth was in great demand. Blundells, the famous public school, is also located in the town. Torrington, with its breezy hilltop location, was noted for its castle. Glovemaking was an important local trade.

One thing that all these towns have in common is a market. Some of the original charters go back hundreds of years, and the markets themselves are held in equally ancient market halls. Some suffered in the last century when the railways brought goods and supplies in from the outside world, but in the latter half of the 20th century they have made a spirited come-back, and are thriving again.

Barnstaple, The Bridge 1890 24858

The Long Bridge over the broad waters of the River Taw was certainly built by 1300, but it may be a hundred years or more older. With sixteen stone arches, much of the original fabric survives after a widening in 1796. That it survives at all, carrying the volume of traffic that uses it today, speaks volumes for the skill of the ancient stonemasons.

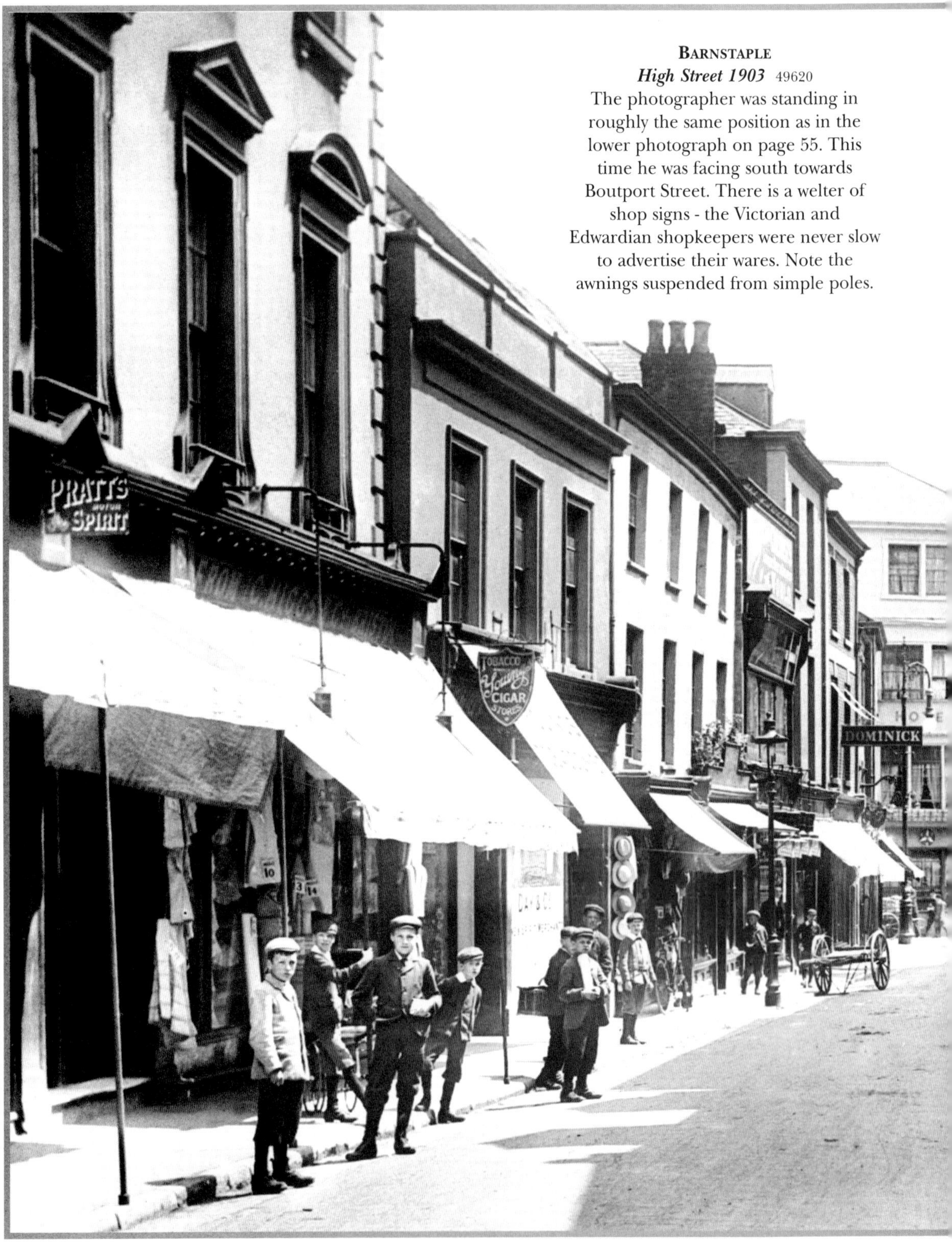

BARNSTAPLE
High Street 1903 49620
The photographer was standing in roughly the same position as in the lower photograph on page 55. This time he was facing south towards Boutport Street. There is a welter of shop signs - the Victorian and Edwardian shopkeepers were never slow to advertise their wares. Note the awnings suspended from simple poles.

BROOKS'
CAFÉ
PRATT'S
SPIRIT
101
OPTICIAN

BARNSTAPLE, THE SQUARE 1903 49616

The Square lies at the north end of the Long Bridge. The building to the right is the red façade of The Athenaeum, built in 1888, which houses the museum and a collection of fossils. The gazebo was provided as a shelter for the horse-drawn cab drivers, who are plying for business alongside.

BARNSTAPLE, THE SQUARE 1935 86654

This photograph was taken from an almost identical spot. A few cosmetic changes to the buildings can be seen, several of which have been combined to form Prideaux's garage. They are still in business, but on a different site. A roundabout has replaced the gazebo, and trees have been flattened behind the Albert Clock to improve road visibility. The building thus revealed is the Imperial Hotel.

BARNSTAPLE
The Athenaeum 1906
This view shows the end of Boutport Street, where it enters The Square. The large building in the distance is The Athenaeum. On the left is the Golden Lion Hotel, with its attractive twin shallow bays and decorative wrought-iron balcony.

BARNSTAPLE
High Street 1894
The town has a long commercial history, and was once the home of many prosperous textile merchants. In this view of the High Street, looking north, we see a pleasing medley of old and new, the Georgian buildings standing shoulder to shoulder with later Victorian infill.

BARNSTAPLE, THE ATHENAEUM 1906 56044

BARNSTAPLE, HIGH STREET 1894 33422

BARNSTAPLE
Butchers' Row 1919 69323
The delightful open-fronted small shops are still largely unchanged today. On the left is the Pannier Market, built in 1885, a grand construction with a wooden vaulted roof of cathedral-like proportions. Market Days are Tuesday and Friday. Friday is also Cattle Market day, and the town heaves with people, augmented in summer by visitors.

MOULE
C.H.BALMENT
SLEE
SLEE

HONITON, HIGH STREET AND ST PAUL'S CHURCH 1904 52109
Honiton is renowned for its lace, and the royal christening robe, still in use today, was made here for Queen Victoria in 1841. The building on the right, opposite the church, is now used as a lace museum. Many of the pleasing late Georgian buildings in this picture are still standing.

HONITON, HIGH STREET c1955 H111039
The High Street again, and a much busier scene is shown. The road is the A30 London to the west of England road which, even in 1955, could become horribly congested, especially at summer weekends. This broad thoroughfare runs the entire length of the town.

Honiton, A Laceworker 1907 58075
One of the last bobbin lace makers at work. The industry started around the time of Queen Elizabeth I, and by 1700 there were the astonishing number of 4,695 people in the area engaged in the trade. Even by 1852, there were still 4,101. With the arrival of machines the trade disintegrated.

Honiton, New Street 1904 52110

Honiton

New Street 1904 52110

After taking the upper picture on page 58, the photographer turned right into New Street to create this evocative image. The Methodist chapel is on the left, whilst ahead is a railway bridge. The station is to the right, on the old London and South Western Railway line from Waterloo to Exeter.

Newton Abbot

The Market 1925 78550

The original Charter for this busy market was given around 1250 at the time the town became a borough. Drovers urge their animals through the throng, farmers haggle, and the townspeople watch out for bargains. Honiton's population exploded during Victorian times, owing to its importance as a rail junction.

Newton Abbot, The Market 1925 78550

Newton Abbot, Courtenay Park 1906 56576
Located just across the road from the train station, the park is named after the Courtenays, who were responsible for much of the building in town (they owned most of the land). A spacious recreation area, it is surrounded by elegant villas, mostly Italianate in style.

Newton Abbot, from Decoy 1906 56571
Another open area of Newton Abbot is Decoy, to the south of town. With playing fields, a recreation area, a lake and woodlands, it is very popular with the local townspeople. There are fine views over the town and to the wooded slopes beyond.

NEWTON ABBOT, THE GLOBE HOTEL & ST LEONARD'S TOWER 1906 56573

A party of guests has boarded a coach outside The Globe Hotel, probably to enjoy a day's excursion to Torquay or the wilds of Dartmoor. The hotel is now reduced in status to a furniture warehouse. St Leonard's Tower, smothered in ivy, is all that remains of a fourteenth century church, demolished in 1836.

OKEHAMPTON, FORE STREET MARKET 1890 22590
Okehampton was established near a Saxon site just after the Norman conquest. The church in the picture is St James. This was built as a chantry chapel to All Saints, which was in the Saxon part of the town, well away from the newer area. Farmers gather at the corner to mull over the issues of the day.

OKEHAMPTON, MELDON VIADUCT 1906 56058
The London and South Western Railway built their Exeter to Plymouth line to the north of Dartmoor through Okehampton. At Meldon, it crossed the West Okement River on this 120-feet high cast iron structure, opened in 1874. The line is now closed, although tracks still service a local quarry and Bere Alston.

TAVISTOCK, WEST STREET 1922 73204
Tavistock is an ancient stannary town, renowned for its 10th-century Benedictine abbey. It was once the largest producer of tin in Europe. After this industry declined it turned to cloth. In the nineteenth century, copper took over - the Great Consols copper mine is nearby. Here we see a pleasing mixture of slate-hung and brick buildings.

TAVISTOCK, DUKE STREET 1890 22546
The delicate spire on the left was the Methodist church and is now demolished. The local constable poses stiffly in the left foreground. He may well have been a busy man - Tavistock had a reputation as a somewhat rough mining community, and the centre on Saturday nights could get a little lively.

Tavistock, Duke Street 1910 62256
This photograph looks in the opposite direction to number 22546. The church is St Eustace, one of only two in the country dedicated to this saint. The Churchwardens' Accounts date back to 1385, and are amongst the earliest in England. On the left is the classic small town grocer's, its windows heaving with tins, jars and bottles.

Tavistock, Brook Street 1910 62259
This gently curving street is to the east of the town. This view, looking back towards the town centre, shows both the Congregational and parish churches. The latter has three spectacular aisles, one built for the ancient Clothworkers' Guild with a roof of finely-carved beams and bosses.

TIVERTON, THE PARK 1903 49612

TIVERTON

The Park 1903

Tiverton is well blessed with open green spaces. With an old castle, and the River Exe running through the town, it presents plenty of opportunities for recreation. Here, family groups enjoy the sunshine and an old man sits alongside an ancient cannon.

TIVERTON

St Paul's Street 1920

This view looks towards the church from West Exe North. Set in an area of Victorian factory housing, these streets of modest but pleasing terraces are now part of a Conservation Area. Penny's, the corner shop, offers not only newspapers but fancy goods and a library.

TIVERTON, ST PAUL'S STREET 1920 69889

TIVERTON, CASTLE STREET 1920 69888

Castle Street runs north from the town centre. Two boys are using the drainage dyke to sail their toy yacht. The town was once a significant cloth-producing centre, renowned for its kersey. After the decline in its fortunes, the town found new prosperity through John Heathcoat's foundries, sawmills and agricultural machinery factory.

TORRINGTON, CASTLE HILL 1890 24842

Castle Hill is part of 365 acres of common land donated for "...the relief of the poor" in the 12th century. There are 20 miles of public rights of way. The river Torridge is to the left, and the straight line just to the right of it is the old course of the Rolle (or Great Torrington) canal.

TORRINGTON, MAILIN BRIDGE 1890 24844
Another view from Castle Hill, this time looking west. In the bottom left corner is the tramway that brought ball clay from Peters Marland to the station at Torrington (centre). This was finally made into a main line in the 1920s with passenger services to Halwill Junction. It closed less than 40 years later.

TORRINGTON, MARKET PLACE 1893 32334
The gothic-style drinking fountain was presented to the town by the Honorable Mark Rolle in 1870. Beyond, the elegant arcade belongs to the Town Hall, jutting out into the street on stone piers, built in 1861. Torrington's prosperity was founded on wool.

Totnes, High Street 1896 38228

The ancient town of Totnes was once second only to Exeter as a prosperous merchants' town, but declined in importance in the 19th century. This is the south end of the High Street, with the ramparts of its ruined castle visible in the middle of the picture. Totnes had a medieval wall around the centre, much of it still intact.

TOTNES, BUTTERWALK 1896 38227
A lower view of the High Street. The covered walks, created by overhanging stories, were the location of two historic parts of the market area. On the right is the colonnaded and heavily shaded Butterwalk; to the left is Birdwalk. Butter was sold in the former, poultry in the latter.

TOTNES, THE 'TOTNES CASTLE' 1896 38216
The river Dart is one of the many delights of Totnes. Here a paddle steamer reverses off the landing stage. Trips down the river were as common then as they are today. It is regrettable that steam has given way to the internal combustion engine. Note the covered carriages waiting on shore.

The Cities

DESPITE ITS large area, Devon has only two cities, Plymouth in the west and Exeter in the east. Both are old, both enjoy fascinating histories, and both suffered extensive bomb damage during the Second World War. Plymouth is the larger of the two, and Exeter the more ancient.

The use of 'Plymouth' as a name originates from the 13th century. Before then it was called Sutton, a name that survives today. As England's naval might grew, so did the need for a sheltered, deep-water anchorage, which Plymouth provided. Houses and facilities for the ships and men to crew them developed. The Barbican district, that was home to Drake, Raleigh and a band of other swashbucklers and privateers, still exists to this day. As England's most westerly port, Plymouth was the place where our navy lay in wait for the Spanish Armada. The famous Hoe is still to be seen, where Drake played bowls while he waited for the arrival of the enemy. In fact, as the tide was flooding and the wind against him, he would not have been able to move earlier. Drake began his circumnavigation of the world from here in 1577; the Pilgrim Fathers set sail for the New World; Cook in 1768 to chart New Zealand; Charles Darwin set off in the Beagle in 1831. For a century, Millbay Dock was the destination of transatlantic liners. It was quicker to put in at Plymouth and transfer passengers to trains for London than it was to sail on to Southampton. By 1941, the naval dockyards and much of the ancient centre had been obliterated by German bombs. As much of our navy was based here, it was deemed a legitimate target.

Despite having no real military significance, Exeter also suffered in the War. In May 1942, the Luftwaffe attacked the city. Much of the centre was razed and over 400 shops and 36 pubs and clubs were destroyed. Exeter was once a Roman fortification, and can lay claim to a much longer history than Plymouth. Some of the original Roman walls have been discovered and can still be seen today. The city was arguably the first town in England to be served by a canal with locks. Opened in 1566, it made it possible for sea-going ships to reach the city centre. The canal was always smaller than commercial and shipping interests would have liked, though its size was increased several times over the centuries. The commercial traffic lasted until 31st December 1998.

EXETER, MOL'S COFFEE HOUSE 1906 53783

The elaborate Elizabethan structure in the centre, with tiers of multi-paned windows and a high gallery, was the renowned Mol's Coffee House, standing beside Cathedral Green. It was reputed to have been a meeting place for Drake and Hawkins. Alongside is the tiny church of St Martin.

EXETER, THE CATHEDRAL 1924 76579

Exeter's spacious cathedral is thirteenth century with earlier Norman towers. It suffered during the Dissolution and again at the hands of Cromwell's men. After two centuries of neglect, Sir Gilbert Scott restored it in the 1870s. The interior is magnificent with a breathtakingly beautiful ribbed vault.

EXETER, HIGH STREET 1900 46043

These tall commercial buildings are still there today, marred somewhat by new frontages. Exeter was the furthest west that the Romans ventured. They halted on the banks of the Exe in about 50AD and founded the town of Isca. The West Country see was transferred to the safety of the Exeter city walls in 1049.

VICTORIA
PALACE
THE VICTORIA
BOOT PALACE
178. R. P. ACOTT. 178
NETT CASH PRICES
HOSKINS & SON
MACHINE BREAD BAKERS
AND
CONFECTIONERS.

Exeter

Fore Street 1896 38008

The High Street becomes Fore Street as it heads down towards the river Exe. The street today is a mass of shops and attractive buildings, none more so than Tuckers Hall. This delightful building with its stone-mullioned windows is a reminder of the days when wool played an important role in the local economy.

EXETER, HIGH STREET AND GUILDHALL 1929 82291
Another view of the High Street. The exquisite Guildhall is in the centre. It was built in 1330, remodelled in 1468, and the portico over the pavement added in 1592. The electric tram service, the tracks for which stretch along the road, was inaugurated in 1905.

EXETER, EXE BRIDGE 1929 82300
At that time, Exe Bridge was all that was needed to deal with Exeter's traffic. Today, a parallel bridge has been built, creating an enormous roundabout. A trolley bus is threading its way over into the city.

Exeter, Stepcote Hill 1911 63678

Stepcote Hill links Exeter city with the Exe valley, and is unchanged today. At the bottom is 'The House that Moved': this historic local building was in the path of a road scheme, and was carefully excavated and rolled some 400 yards to a new position.

EXETER, FROM THE CANAL 1896 38033

Exeter's canal was built at the request of the Tudor merchants, who were exasperated by the weirs on the Exe that obstructed their vessels. It opened in 1566, and boasted the first pound locks in Britain. Originally just 16 feet wide, it was widened in the 1820s by James Green.

EXETER, THE PORT 1896 38034

Graceful sailing ships are clustered alongside the quay on the Exeter Canal at the north end. The warehouse and Customs buildings around the Basin and riverside are beautifully preserved. In the background the city buildings rise over the rooftops.

PLYMOUTH, THE GUILDHALL AND POST OFFICE 1889 22388
The impressive Guildhall, a masterpiece of elaborate Victorian Gothic, was built in 1874. There had been three other such buildings previously. During the last war it was reduced to a mere shell but has since been restored to its original glory. Its tower is a noted landmark over the city.

PLYMOUTH, GEORGE STREET 1889 22397
George Street was once the very heart of the old city but was almost entirely destroyed in the blitz. Today, a short section behind the Theatre Royal is all that is left. Here the broad thoroughfare is thronged with carts, cabs and omnibuses. In the background are the offices of the Great Western Railway.

STEVENS
STOMS & INSURANCE
AGENT
AND
SHIP BROKER
DURANT'S
BRUNSWICK HOTEL.
60PH

PLYMOUTH
The Barbican 1890 22474
This picturesque area of narrow streets sits alongside the ancient fishing quay of Sutton's Pool. From here crowds watched the departure of the Pilgrim Fathers' vessel 'Mayflower' in 1620 on its voyage to the New World. The city's fish market was located here until the late 1990s, when it moved across the harbour to a new purpose-built dock.

PLYMOUTH, THE CLOCK TOWER 1892 30597

This view shows the same scene as the lower photograph on page 79, but three years later. Derry's Clock Tower was given to the city in 1862 and was known for years as the 'four-faced deceiver' - this because the fountain on each side had no water. To its right a new elaborate office building has been constructed on the corner.

PLYMOUTH, OLD TOWN STREET 1889 22398

In this busy scene Victorian ladies shelter from the sun under dark parasols. They must have been sweltering in their heavy gowns. Old Town Street, like so many Plymouth thoroughfares, was devastated in the war. Altogether, around twenty thousand Plymouth buildings were destroyed as a result of enemy bombing.

Plymouth
Tavistock Road 1890

School children linger on the pavements close by their school. Each boy wears a smart suit and cap or boater, each girl a bright white pinafore dress. New substantial terraced buildings mark the march of the residential area out of the old city into the fields outside.

Plymouth
Bedford Street 1904

Bedford Street is another road that disappeared from the map following the blitz. It is clear that the Victorians remodelled much of the old city, constructing public and commercial buildings on a grand scale. Styled mostly in the preferred ornate Gothic, these additions sit awkwardly among the older, more urbane 18th-century buildings.

Plymouth, Tavistock Road 1890 22423

Plymouth, Bedford Street 1904 52407

PLYMOUTH, UNION STREET 1904 52406

Union Street was more fortunate than many of its neighbours and escaped the worst of the bombing. This view shows the tram tracks that spread along the city's main thoroughfares. On the left is Oliver's, one of the early chainstores, offering cheap boots and shoes.

PLYMOUTH, THE LIDO 1934 86216

The Lido and the walks were popular with the Victorians, and they offer beautiful views across the Sound. The lighthouse was rebuilt there, having been superseded by a more efficient building on the Eddystone rock south of the harbour. Close by is the world-famous Hoe.

Plymouth, Onion Sellers 1907 59208

Two young lads stand by the harbour wall with their strings of onions. With their grimy jackets and trousers, they give every impression of having endured an uncomfortable passage. For many years, Plymouth, with its direct ferry service to Brittany, saw French onion sellers in the town every year.

Devonport, Halfpenny Bridge 1904 52427

The attractive Halfpenny Bridge is so named because of the charge to cross it. Today, the whole area is unrecognizable, some of the creek has been filled in, the ramshackle huts demolished, and the banks are the home of leisure boat builders.

The County's Backwaters

ONE OF the real delights when visiting Devon is exploring its remote lanes, to discover villages that have watched the twentieth century pass by. Modern services may have been installed, and the motor car may have cast its ugly blight on much of the countryside, but still these remote corners remain.

Despite the close proximity of the Torbay coast with its millions of holidaymakers, just a few miles inland you can discover the peace and solitude of the classic English village. Harbertonford, Broadhempston, Denbury - these are the stuff of picture postcards and chocolate box lids. If old cob buildings and acres of thatch are not to your taste, travel a few miles further north to the forbidding expanse of Dartmoor. The terrain may be more rugged, but it possesses a beauty of its own. It is possible to spend the day on the Moor without seeing another living soul. Here there are sturdy bridges and old quarries. The Haytor quarry had its own tramways to move the quarried granite, which was used all over the country, and for some famous buildings - London Bridge was built from Haytor granite.

Dartmoor is the watershed for Devon. Many rivers flow north, making the long journey to the Atlantic Ocean. At Belstone, on the north face of the moor, there is a pleasant walk along the banks of the river Taw, which flows through several delightful villages on its way to Barnstaple. A mile to the west, the East Okement River, a tiny stream at this stage, flows into the Torridge, which then takes a circuitous route to Bideford. Below the town, Taw and Torridge meet off Appledore before emptying their combined waters into the sea. The Tamar rises just three miles from the north coast and heads south all the way to Plymouth, its snaking course forming most of the county boundary with Cornwall.

The villages of north Devon may be a little more Spartan than their southern counterparts, but that reflects the difference in climate. North Devonians tend to look somewhat askance at their softer southern neighbours. But villages like Croyde, Simonsbath and Brayford also have their fair share of thatched cottages and narrow lanes.

To the east, the rivers Exe, Otter and Axe all have their green fertile plains and individual charm. It would be hard not to be moved by such delightful places as Gittisham, Ottery St Mary and Sidbury.

Devon presents one obstacle to exploring its hidden treasures: wherever you roam off the beaten track in Devon, you will drive along lanes with high embankments and blind bends, only wide enough for one car. If you are driving you must concentrate on the road and not the landscape. It is better by far to travel on foot or by bicycle so as to enjoy this wonderful county to the full.

IVYBRIDGE, FROM THE RIVER C1886 8304
A view in winter of the river Erme near Ivybridge. This pretty river rises on Dartmoor, seen in the background, and flows 14 miles to the English Channel. It once provided water power to grist and paper mills en route.

IVYBRIDGE, GENERAL VIEW 1890 22517

IVYBRIDGE
General View 1890

Ivybridge was a modest town when this view was taken. Now it is a dormitory for Plymouth, and has grown dramatically in recent years. The Great Western line between Exeter and Plymouth crosses the valley on a graceful viaduct, and this can be seen in the distance.

IVYBRIDGE
The Old Church 1890

Many country churches went into decline in the Victorian era. Roofs fell in, walls collapsed through the weight of smothering ivy, and congregations declined. This neglect would not be tolerated in our own conservation-conscious age. Ivybridge was built astride the main road from Plymouth to Exeter.

IVYBRIDGE, THE OLD CHURCH 1890 22522

IVYBRIDGE, THE BRIDGE c1955 122043.
The river Erme tumbles down and makes its way through the village. Ivybridge was a popular destination for day trips for the workers of Plymouth. There are two bridges here, one carrying the road to Exeter and the other the road to Cornwood.

CHAGFORD, MARKET PLACE 1906 56609
Chagford is a tiny market town on the eastern slopes of Dartmoor, close to the upper reaches of the river Teign. With its jumble of streets and pleasing buildings of local moorstone, it has long been popular with visitors. Alongside the market place is the renowned Three Crowns Inn, where the poet Sidney Godolphin was shot during the Civil War.

PRINCETOWN, STREET SCENE 1931 84058
'A grey town and a grim town, pervaded with the unlovely spirit of its fearful prison.' Thus Arthur Mee captures the forbidding character of this remote community, beset by fogs and rain. It came into being 200 years ago when granite was being quarried. The land was given by the Prince of Wales, and from him it gained its name.

PRINCETOWN, DARTMOOR PRISON GATE AND CONVICTS 1890 22578
Dartmoor Prison at Princetown was built in 1806, initially to house French prisoners of war. Its closure in 1816 saw Princetown virtually abandoned, but the arrival of a railway for the granite quarries in 1823 brought salvation. The prison re-opened in 1850 and has since housed some of our most hardened criminals.

Widecombe in the Moor 1907 5805
This tiny hamlet, tucked high up in the East Webburn river valley, huddles about its central green. St Pancras Church, with its lofty pinnacled tower, was built in granite in the 14th century. It was to come to Widecombe Fair that Uncle Tom Cobley borrowed Tom Pearce's grey mare.

Dartmoor, Warren House Inn 1931 84044
Many a stranded traveller has had cause to thank The Warren House Inn at Postbridge. It sits high on Dartmoor, alongside the Moretonhampstead to Princetown road, near where the East Dart river rises. The bleak moorland road to Moretonhampstead stretches out into the distance.

BOVEY TRACEY, THE COACH FOR THE MOORS 1907 58522
This pleasant little town is perched on a hillside above the river Bovey. It was on the railway from Newton Abbot to Moretonhampstead, but the line closed to passengers on 28th February 1959. The Posting House on the right is a reminder of the earlier age of horse-drawn transport.

Kingsbridge, Fore Street and Bank 1896 38507
This old town is at the heart of a region of fertile farming country known as the South Hams. This view looks down the main street towards the tidal estuary extending up from Salcombe. The street is lined with a wide variety of buildings, including slate-hung houses with fine period shopfronts.

Kingsbridge, Fore Street 1896 38429
This view is looking up Fore Street towards the parish church of St Thomas Becket. It is said that this church was built as a penance by William Tracy for his part in Becket's murder. The railway wrought considerable change when it arrived in the town in 1893 and holidaymakers discovered its attractions.

KINGSBRIDGE, THE PROMENADE 1920 69824
A paddle steamer loaded with trippers has just left for a voyage down the estuary. Steamers like this were a feature of many harbours in Victorian times, offering the first pleasure service to eager holidaymakers. Until the 19th century Kingsbridge was an important port for the shipping of wool and foundry products.

KINGSBRIDGE, THE BRIDGE 1890 24525
To the east of Kingsbridge is the road to Torcross and Slapton Sands. This photograph shows the old four-arched bridge over the estuary. There has been a crossing here since the 10th century. In the background, hedges snake their way up over the slopes.

ASHBURTON, TOWN CENTRE 1904 51202
The town lies just inside the Dartmoor National Park alongside the main Exeter to Plymouth road. Once stage coaches thundered through, forcing bystanders onto the narrow pavements. In grander and more prosperous days Ashburton was one of the region's strategic stannary towns. Mining finally came to a halt in the 19th century.

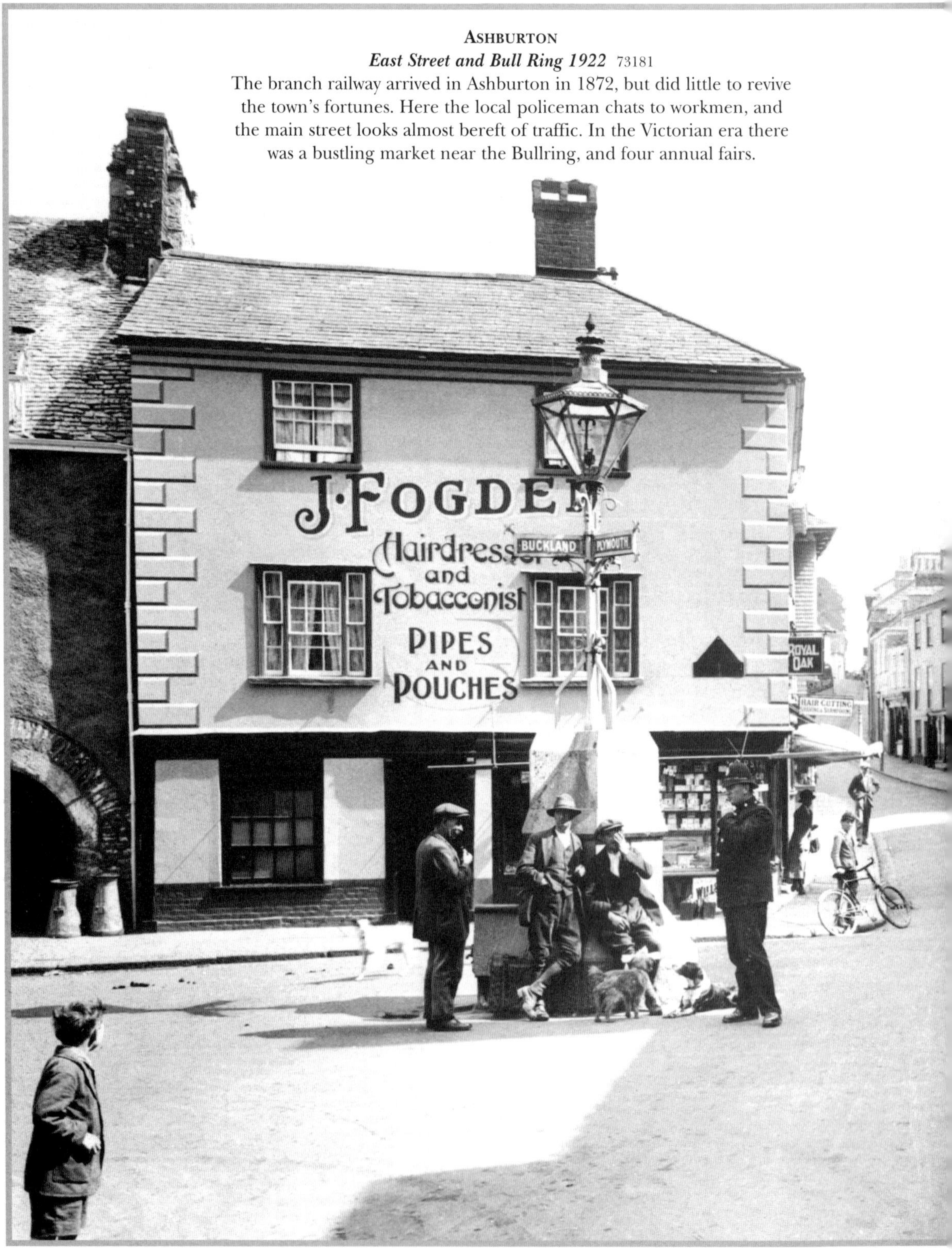

ASHBURTON

East Street and Bull Ring 1922 73181

The branch railway arrived in Ashburton in 1872, but did little to revive the town's fortunes. Here the local policeman chats to workmen, and the main street looks almost bereft of traffic. In the Victorian era there was a bustling market near the Bullring, and four annual fairs.

GARAGE
LLOYDS BANK LIMITED
BRUSH
LAMASON. MANUFACTURE
RAC

ALFINGTON, NEAR OTTERY ST MARY 1906 56678

Alfington is a tiny village alongside the river Otter, north of Ottery St Mary. The narrow lane winds between thatched cottages, the fine example in the foreground featuring a tall chimney to carry the hot smoke safely away.

OTTERY ST MARY, MARKET PLACE 1907 58182

Set in the midst of particularly fertile part of the county, Ottery had a market for centuries. John Coleridge was the Ottery vicar in the 18th century and his son, the poet Samuel Taylor Coleridge ('Rime of the Ancient Mariner' and 'Kubla Khan') went to school here. The awnings are down over the windows; it is a hot, sunny day.

East Budleigh, The Village 1938 88622
It is hard to believe now, but East Budleigh was a port before the river Otter silted up around the sixteenth century. Sir Walter Raleigh was born just outside East Budleigh at Hayes Barton in 1552. All Saints Church is a fifteenth century building. The Raleigh pew, with the family's arms dated 1537, is inside.

Axminster, Trinity Square 1902 48453
There was a minster here as early as 705. Well before that, the Roman Fosse Way threaded its way through the town. In later years stage coaches halted at the 18th-century George Inn. Axminster is famed for its carpet business, founded in 1755 by Thomas Whitty. Manufacture ceased in 1835 but began again in 1937.

The North Coast

WITHOUT question, the north coast of Devon is an area of stark rugged beauty. You have only to study the map to see that seaside towns are not plentiful. Westward Ho! and Ilfracombe are the only two significant resorts on eighty-plus miles of rugged coast, with rocky inlets at Clovelly and Lynmouth. There are also long surf-drenched beaches at Saunton and Woolacombe, some delightful fishing villages, and even a small port at Bideford. All these combine to create a coastline of scenic variety.

North Devon has long appealed to the artistic temperament, particularly to writers. The area around Lynton features extensively in R.D.Blackmore's novel 'Lorna Doone'. Charles Kingsley, best known for 'The Water Babies' and 'Westward Ho!', spent his childhood in Clovelly and wrote some of his books in Bideford.

Henry Williamson, author of the much-loved 'Tarka the Otter', lived at Georgeham near Croyde. In it he included many references to this part of the world. The young Tarka lives and plays around the 'Canal Bridge', an aqueduct of the Torrington Canal, which can still be seen. John Gay, author of 'The Beggar's Opera', was a north Devon man, and several notable actors and stars of the entertainment world live in the area. The leading cricket umpire David Shepherd was born, bred and still lives in Instow. Other visitors to the north coast included the banker Thomas Coutts; the publisher Sir George Newnes came to live in Lynton, and was responsible for the opening of a railway from Barnstaple, which finally opened Lynton to the outside world.

Only two railways penetrated into north Devon: the Southern line from Exeter, and the Great Western from Taunton. The prestigious Atlantic Coast Express had through-coaches to Ilfracombe, and the Devon Belle Pullman service also used the line. All that is left today is a branch line from Exeter to Barnstaple. With a new single carriageway road from the M5 to Barnstaple, north Devon is easier to reach than before, but the local way of life has remained unaffected. The hurry and bustle normally associated with life today is far less here than in Britain's more populated areas.

CLOVELLY, THE HARBOUR 1890 24770
Clovelly is the original picture postcard village, clinging to a steep wooded valley prohibited to motor vehicles. It was largely unknown to the world until Charles Kingsley and Charles Dickens wrote about it. Since then, its fame has become legendary.

CLOVELLY, FROM THE HARBOUR 1906 55953
Another view of the picturesque harbour with its 14th-century stone quay. In bygone years the Clovelly fleet put to sea in pursuit of much-prized herring. On the right is a lime-kiln, now in use as a boathouse.

Clovelly
Main Street 1894
Clovelly hangs on the side of the hill, fringed by luxuriant woodland. Donkeys ply up and down the steep-stepped street, carrying goods on panniers. The New Inn is still there, offering rest and refreshment to visitors. Unlike most villages, the whole area is owned by a Trust, who charge visitors a fee.

Westward Ho!
Pebble Ridge 1906
The Pebble Ridge at Westward Ho! has much to commend it as a defence line against the Atlantic Ocean, which rolls relentlessly in its attempt to reclaim Northam Burrows which lie behind. Two miles long and 20ft high, it is a natural defence. Away from this, there are some pleasant stretches of sand.

Clovelly, Main Street 1894 33490

Westward Ho!, Pebble Ridge 1906 55961

APPLEDORE

The Quay 1923 75145

This charming Devon fishing village lies alongside the broad waters of the Torridge River, which swings left just beyond the point to join the Taw and the open sea. Though still in essence a fishing port, there are only a dozen or so boats today, engaging in salmon-netting and deep-sea fishing. The pilot boat for the estuary is also based here.

APPLEDORE, THE QUAY 1923 75148

APPLEDORE

The Quay 1923

Another view of the busy quay. Where the ships are tied up there is now an extended car park. This area was once noted for its shipbuilding, but only one yard survives today, with a sizeable dry dock. Out of sight round a bend in the river is Bideford.

BIDEFORD

The Quay 1890

Bideford, two miles up-river from Appledore, is now the main commercial port in the area. Once the town manufactured and exported cloth and built ships; it imported tobacco and salted cod, and wool from the Continent for the Devon weaving industry. Today the quay is mostly used by the Lundy ferries.

BIDEFORD, THE QUAY 1890 24800

Bideford, Across the River 1899 43077
A view of Kingsley's ' Little White Town' from across the Torridge, at East-the-Water. Bideford's Market Charter was granted in 1272 by Henry III. The Pannier Market Hall is a delightfully ancient building, recently refurbished. The bridge, with its many arches, each of a different span, is 13th-century.

Bideford, Bridge Street 1906 55933
The view is still recognizable nearly a century later, although the houses on the left became a car park after a slum clearance programme in the early 1960s. East-the-Water is the settlement on the far side of the river. The railings must have provided welcome relief for the weary walker.

BIDEFORD, THE QUAY 1919 69331
There was once a railway running down the middle of this street and around the corner at the end. It went to Westward Ho! and Appledore, and ran for sixteen years, closing in March 1917. The quay where ships tied up is on the extreme right.

BIDEFORD, OLD FORD FARM 1890 24806
Old Ford Farm is virtually unchanged today. This is believed to be the oldest building in Bideford, dating from the 14th century. Less than half a mile upstream from Bideford Bridge, it is close by the original river crossing. This photograph encapsulates farming old-style, with hens running free in the yard by the house.

Instow
The Foreshore 1919

Instow is on the Torridge, opposite Appledore. Apart from a reinforced sea wall, this view of Marine Parade is little changed today. Here, visitors await the ferry for Appledore. The village is famous for its cricket club, which was established in the 1820s.

Woolacombe
General View 1899

The village is at the north end of a magnificent two-mile long sandy beach. Until the 1800s this stretch of coast was remote, its splendours familiar only to Ilfracombe fishermen. The roads inland were narrow and uninviting. It was only in the late Victorian era when builders began to throw up lines of villas overlooking the sea that Woolacombe's attractions were discovered.

Instow, The Foreshore 1919 69337

Woolacombe, General View 1899 43130

WOOLACOMBE, SHELL BEACH 1911 63942
Barricane Beach, also known as Shell Beach, is small and difficult to reach. It was given its local name because of the diversity of shells gathered there. The hotels on the cliff above look out towards the island of Lundy almost twenty miles away.

WOOLACOMBE, FROM THE CLIFFS 1911 63938
Barricane Beach is behind the camera, and we see the broad expanse of Woolacombe sands stretching away south towards Croyde. The high ground to the right is Baggy Point, haunt of the peregrine falcon and once a fearsome threat to sailing ships.

Ilfracombe
View from Capstone Hill 1906

This prospect, photographed from Capstone Hill, shows the sheer density of housing created by the Victorians to cater for the influx of visitors every summer. A century before, Ilfracombe had been little more than a modest fishing village, though already the haunt of a few discerning visitors.

Ilfracombe
Capstone Hill and The Parade 1911

The small beach to the left is at Prechers Rock. Before efficient transport links were opened to Ilfracombe, steamers crossed the Severn estuary from South Wales, discharging hundreds of day-trippers into the town. Today, the harbour is used by fishing boats, and in summer the 'Oldenburg' ferries visitors to Lundy.

Ilfracombe, Capstone Hill 1906 56787

Ilfracombe, Capstone Hill and The Parade 1911 63901

ILFRACOMBE, FROM CAPSTONE HILL 1911 63905
Although Ilfracombe is essentially a Victorian town, the elegant terraced houses of Montpellier Place (upper, left of centre) were built in the early 1830s. Space for development was at a premium in the narrow and steep area between the cliffs and hills, and hotels and lodging houses of several storeys were the preferred solution.

ILFRACOMBE, THE PAVILION 1926 79229
The delightful Victoria Pavilion suffered the ravages of time and fire and was demolished in the early 1990s. A jumble of stylistic influences, it encapsulated the careless exuberance of so much of our seaside architecture.

Ilfracombe
The Bandstand 1923
If the billowing empty deck chair is any guide, the wind is whistling up the Bristol Channel and through the Promenade Gardens. The crowds are already gathering around the bandstand for the afternoon matinee. To the left and behind is the Victoria Pavilion.

Ilfracombe
The Harbour c1890
The outer pier, which provides access to Ilfracombe at any state of the tide, was not yet constructed. In this view, a pleasure steamer is berthed at the quay. The small building at the far end of the quay, below Lantern Hill, with the small chapel on top, is the lifeboat station.

Ilfracombe, The Bandstand 1923 74948

Ilfracombe, The Harbour c1890 I50001

LYNTON, THE VALLEY OF THE ROCKS HOTEL 1907 59372
This famous hotel was built in 1807. The driver blows his horn and Copp's coach 'Defiance' is ready to leave for Barnstaple. By the time of this photograph the narrow gauge railway from Barnstaple had reached Lynton, and the old coaching service was retained purely for holidaymakers.

Lynton, The Valley of the Rocks 1907 59384
This 'convulsion of nature', close by Lynton, was highly popular with Victorian artists and writers, and other early seekers after the sublime and picturesque. Huge rocks lean precariously, the many stacks forming fantastic shapes that worked on the poetic fancy of early visitors like Wordsworth and Coleridge.

Lynmouth, The Pier 1899 43095
The pier was 18th-century, and the Rhenish tower added early in the 1800s by a General Rawdon. Here in the little town, hemmed in all sides by majestic cliffs and headlands, the twin rivers of the Lyn join together and race noisily out into the sea. Shelley praised Lynmouth's unique scenic splendour in 1812.

Lynmouth

Cherry Bridge 1907 59424

In this delightful rural scene, thatched cottages, sheep dogs and a babe-in-arms conjure up images of an earlier, more peaceful age. The sheep dog lies in the dust of the lane welcoming the brief respite from his labour, caused by the chance meeting with the Frith photographer.

LYNMOUTH, EAST AND WEST LYN 1911 63855
Lynmouth's twin rivers run fast and furious, and no more so than in 1952, when it suffered a terrible tragedy. A violent storm broke over Exmoor, and torrents of water hurtled through the streets of the town carrying all before them. More than thirty people lost their lives and the town was devastated.

Lynmouth, The Harbour c1930 L126301

Ships from South Wales carrying lime and coal were once regular visitors to the town. Paddle steamers from Bristol anchored out in the bay bringing trippers to enjoy the breezy heights of Lynton and Countisbury. Along the street in the picture was a special bath house, as well as a number of new hotels and lodgings.

Combe Martin, Schooner in Harbour 1935 86745

Tucked away among 'surroundings that are indescribably beautiful', boats nestle in the placid harbour waters of this picturesque village with its long, straggling street. Combe Martin's climate has been praised: 'A stay here is wonderfully beneficial to those suffering from threatened lung trouble'.

COMBE MARTIN
View of the Village 1930 83463

Index

Appledore 104-105, 106
Ashburton 95, 96-97
Axminster 99
Babbacombe 32
Barnstaple 51, 52-53, 54, 55, 56-57
Beer 17, 18
Bideford 106, 107, 108
Bovey Tracey 92
Bovisand 49
Brixham 39, 40, 41, 42-43
Budleigh Salterton 23, 24
Chagford 89
Clovelly 101, 102, 103
Combe Martin 119, 120-121
Dartmoor 91
Dartmouth 44, 45
Dawlish 28, 29
Devonport 85
East Budleigh 99
Exeter 72, 73, 74-75, 76, 77, 78
Exmouth 25
Honiton 58, 59, 60
Hope 48
Ilfracombe 111, 112, 113
Instow 109
Ivybridge 87, 88, 89
Kingsbridge 93, 94, 95
Lynmouth 115, 116-117, 118, 119
Lynton 114, 115
Newton Abbot 60, 61, 62
Okehampton 63
Ottery St Mary 98
Paignton 35, 36-37, 38
Plymouth 79, 80-81, 82, 83, 84, 85
Princetown 90
Salcombe 46, 47
Seaton 15
Sidmouth 19, 20-21, 22
Tavistock 64, 65
Teignmouth 30, 31
Tiverton 66, 67
Topsham 26-27
Torquay 33, 34
Torrington 67, 68
Totnes 69, 70
Westward Ho! 103
Widecombe in the Moor 91
Woolacombe 109, 110

To receive your FREE Mounted Print

Cut out this Voucher and return it with your remittance for £1.50 to cover postage and handling. Choose any photograph included in this book. Your SEPIA print will be A4 in size, and mounted in a cream mount with burgundy rule lines, overall size 14 x 11 inches.

Order additional Mounted Prints at HALF PRICE (only £7.49 each*)

If there are further pictures you would like to order, possibly as gifts for friends and family, acquire them at half price (no additional postage and handling required).

Have your Mounted Prints framed*

For an additional £14.95 per print you can have your chosen Mounted Print framed in an elegant polished wood and gilt moulding, overall size 16 x 13 inches (no additional postage and handling required).

*** IMPORTANT!**
These special prices are only available if ordered using the original voucher on this page (no copies permitted) and at the same time as your free Mounted Print, for delivery to the same address

Voucher for FREE and Reduced Price Frith Prints

Picture no.	Page number	Qty	Mounted @ £7.49	Framed + £14.95	Total Cost
		1	**Free of charge***	£	£
			£	£	£
			£	£	£
			£	£	£
			£	£	£
			£	£	£
				* Post & handling	£1.50
				Total Order Cost	**£**

Title: DEVON
052-7

Please do not photocopy this voucher. Only the original is valid, so please cut it out and return it to us.

I enclose a cheque / postal order for £ . . . .
made payable to 'The Francis Frith Collection'
OR please debit my Mastercard / Visa / Switch / Amex card

Number . . . .

Expires . . . . Signature . . . .

Name Mr/Mrs/Ms ....

Address ....

....

....

....

.... Postcode ....

Daytime Tel No ....

Valid to 31/12/01

Frith Collectors' Guild

From time to time we publish a magazine of news and stories about Frith photographs and further special offers of Frith products. If you would like 12 months FREE membership, please return this form and we will send you a New Member Pack.

Send completed forms to:
The Francis Frith Collection, Frith's Barn, Teffont, Salisbury, Wiltshire SP3 5QP

The Francis Frith Collectors' Guild

I would like to receive the New Members Pack offering 12 months FREE membership.

052-7

Name Mr/Mrs/Ms ....

Address ....

....

....

.... Postcode ....

Frith Book Co 1999 Titles

From 2000 we aim at publishing 100 new books each year. For latest catalogue please contact Frith Book Co

Barnstaple	1-85937-084-5	£12.99	Oct 99
Blackpool	1-85937-049-7	£12.99	Sep 99
Bognor Regis	1-85937-055-1	£12.99	Sep 99
Bristol	1-85937-050-0	£12.99	Sep 99
Cambridge	1-85937-092-6	£12.99	Oct 99
Cambridgeshire	1-85937-086-1	£14.99	Nov 99
Cheshire	1-85937-045-4	£14.99	Sep 99
Chester	1-85937-090-X	£12.99	Nov 99
Chesterfield	1-85937-071-3	£12.99	Sep 99
Chichester	1-85937-089-6	£12.99	Nov 99
Cornwall	1-85937-054-3	£14.99	Sep 99
Cotswolds	1-85937-099-3	£14.99	Nov 99

Derby	1-85937-046-2	£12.99	Sep 99
Devon	1-85937-052-7	£14.99	Sep 99
Dorset	1-85937-075-6	£14.99	Oct 99
Dorset Coast	1-85937-062-4	£14.99	Sep 99
Dublin	1-85937-058-6	£12.99	Sep 99
East Anglia	1-85937-059-4	£14.99	Sep 99
Eastbourne	1-85937-061-6	£12.99	Sep 99
English Castles	1-85937-078-0	£14.99	Oct 99
Essex	1-85937-082-9	£14.99	Nov 99
Falmouth	1-85937-066-7	£12.99	Sep 99
Hampshire	1-85937-064-0	£14.99	Sep 99
Hertfordshire	1-85937-079-9	£14.99	Nov 99
Isle of Man	1-85937-065-9	£14.99	Sep 99
Liverpool	1-85937-051-9	£12.99	Sep 99

Maidstone	1-85937-056-X	£12.99	Sep 99
Northumberland & Tyne and Wear	1-85937-072-1	£14.99	Sep 99
North Yorkshire	1-85937-048-9	£14.99	Sep 99
Nottingham	1-85937-060-8	£12.99	Sep 99
Oxfordshire	1-85937-076-4	£14.99	Oct 99
Penzance	1-85937-069-1	£12.99	Sep 99
Reading	1-85937-087-X	£12.99	Nov 99
St Ives	1-85937-068-3	£12.99	Sep 99
Salisbury	1-85937-091-8	£12.99	Nov 99
Scarborough	1-85937-104-3	£12.99	Sep 99
Scottish Castles	1-85937-077-2	£14.99	Oct 99
Sevenoaks and Tonbridge	1-85937-057-8	£12.99	Sep 99
Sheffield and S Yorkshire	1-85937-070-5	£12.99	Sep 99
Shropshire	1-85937-083-7	£14.99	Nov 99
Southampton	1-85937-088-8	£12.99	Nov 99
Staffordshire	1-85937-047-0	£14.99	Sep 99
Stratford upon Avon	1-85937-098-5	£12.99	Nov 99
Suffolk	1-85937-074-8	£14.99	Oct 99
Surrey	1-85937-081-0	£14.99	Oct 99
Torbay	1-85937-063-2	£12.99	Sep 99
Wiltshire	1-85937-053-5	£14.99	Sep 99

British Life A Century Ago
246 x 189mm
144pp, hardback.
Black and white
Lavishly illustrated with photos from the turn of the century, and with extensive commentary. It offers a unique insight into the social history and heritage of bygone Britain.

1-85937-103-5 £17.99 ....

Available from your local bookshop or from the publisher